PRAISE FOR S

What intimate energy Rosemar
poems, which so often record
compelling manner of a modern-day Louis MacNeice. This authentic voice offers moving and vigorous testaments to living through interesting times, both personally and out in the world. The reader will discern Belfast riots, historical offence, and inherited prejudice, with literal events sometimes mirrored in terms of other experiences. Death and love infuse her lines with precision and risk, in arresting and original language. In the extended poem on her father's death, she splices patiently through that defining relationship and its loss. Jenkinson may reveal the facets of the casual quotidian and make them urgent, but such urgencies also accompany her travels into globally heated terrain, among them Ukraine and Tel Aviv. Ever the observer of herself, we encounter moments of intimacy that are deliciously sensual and passionate. Fabulous, essential poems, not just for today but for living with.

– Mary O'Donnell

Rosemary Jenkinson's *Sandy Row Riots* introduces a fearless poet as attuned to the sensuality of life as she is to the complications of death. Widely travelled and circling the East Belfast of her birth with a keen weather eye, Jenkinson peels back layers of history and tribalism to show us the landscape that shapes and has shaped us. A formally inventive, witty, and atmospheric debut.

– Jessica Traynor

Sandy Row Riots is a tour de force; truthful and fearless. Whether the subject is sectarian violence, the celebration of a lover's body, or a visit to the dentist, Jenkinson's ability to capture the reader shines through in vivid images and memorable phrases. The long poem, 'Westward Unbound', is heartbreaking in its honesty and tenderness. This collection is a stunning debut.

– Moyra Donaldson

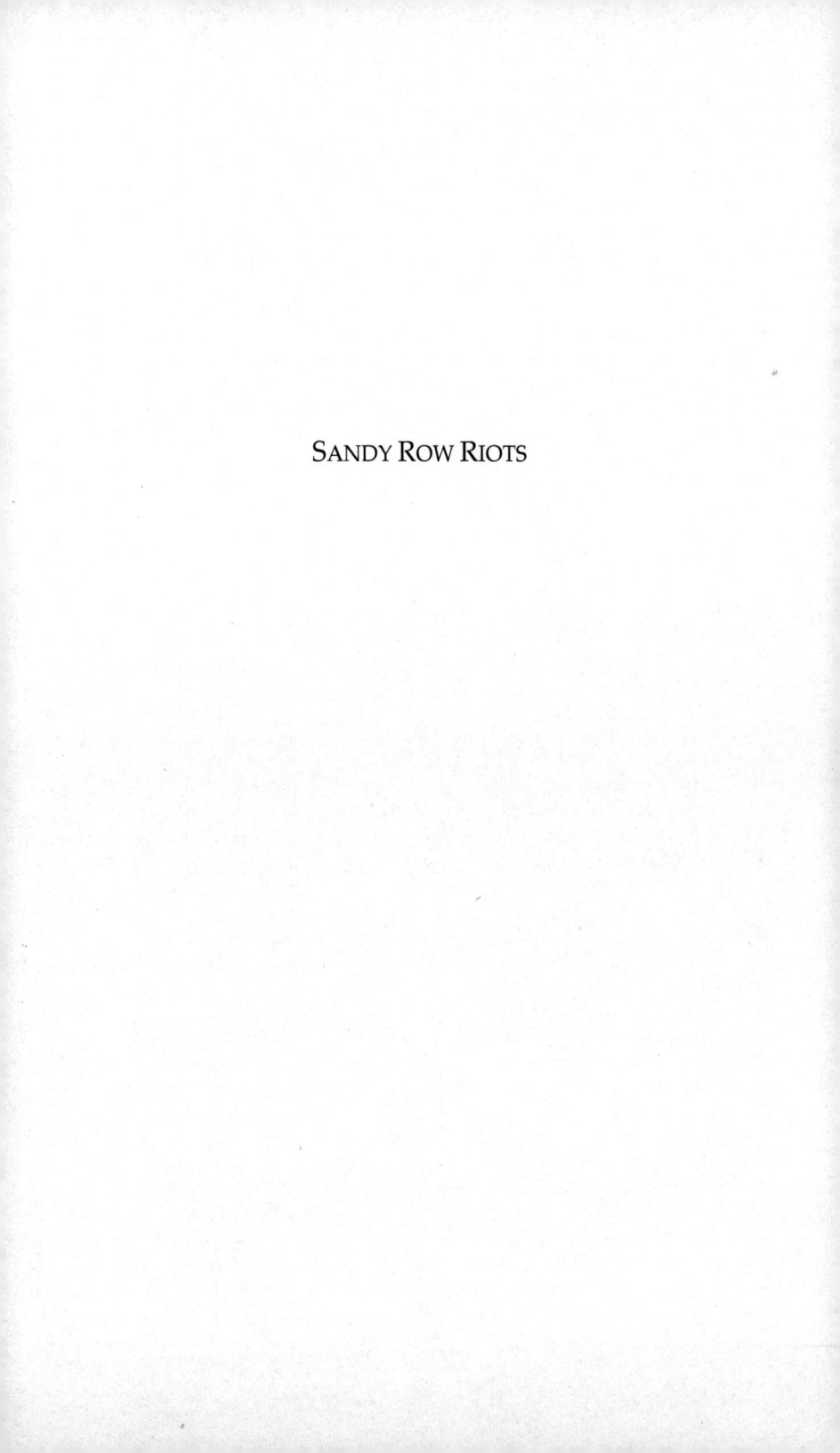

Sandy Row Riots

Rosemary Jenkinson

SANDY ROW RIOTS

Sandy Row Riots

is published in 2024 by
ARLEN HOUSE
42 Grange Abbey Road
Baldoyle
Dublin D13 A0F3
Ireland
Email: arlenhouse@gmail.com
www.arlenhouse.ie

ISBN 978–1–85132–331–9, paperback

International distribution
SYRACUSE UNIVERSITY PRESS
621 Skytop Road, Suite 110
Syracuse
New York 13244–5290
USA
Email: supress@syr.edu
www.syracuseuniversitypress.syr.edu

© Rosemary Jenkinson, 2024

The moral right of the author has been asserted

Typesetting by Arlen House

Cover images by Barry Kerr

Contents

13	After Daniel McColgan's Murder
14	Orchardlands
16	Bukowski Blue
18	The Smile Clinic
19	The Wake at Turf Lodge
21	Belfast
23	The Wand
24	Cregagh Glen in March
25	Heliophile
27	An Aphorism on Divis Mountain
28	Then Suddenly
29	Ravenhill Bonefire
30	Call of the Ancestors
31	Making the Most of the 1912 Suite
32	Hic Jacet
33	Axis Mundi
34	Cuberdon (or The Immutability of Belgian Love)
35	Oceanus
36	Madden's Bar, Castle Court
37	Sandy Row Riots
38	Sham Supermarket, Sandy Row
40	The Pint
41	Choosing the Unbeaten Path
43	The Peacebroker
44	A Belfast Summer
45	Noah Donohoe
46	The Alice Kyteler Girl Gang
47	On the Seabed
48	On Waiting for a Better Day
49	L'Oreille en Rose
50	Christmas Beach Party
52	An Ode to Dangerous Women

54	Willowfield Parade
55	The Courtship
56	White Nights
57	After Intimacy
58	Proverbs for All Writers
59	Half-Dead Poets Society
60	An Illumination in Bittles Bar
61	It's the Animal in Me, Baby
63	December
64	Art
65	Eternity in a Glass
66	Tempus
67	Westward Unbound
74	A Prayer in Kharkiv
75	Cailleach
76	Wintering It Out
77	Walk, Interrupted
79	Blood Queen
80	Nonconformist
81	Being Saved at Whiterock
82	A Playwright Ahead of Her Time
83	Like I was Never There
85	Brexit
86	The Gun that Shot John Caldwell
87	The 6a to the River of Lethe
88	Summer Salt
89	Pommel Horse
91	*Acknowledgements*
92	*About the Author*

'then she injured her neck while doing her yoga
and she went on disability, and again I was glad for her,
all the poets wanted to get disability insurance
it was better than immortality'

– Charles Bukowski, *the angel who pushed his wheelchair*

Sandy Row Riots

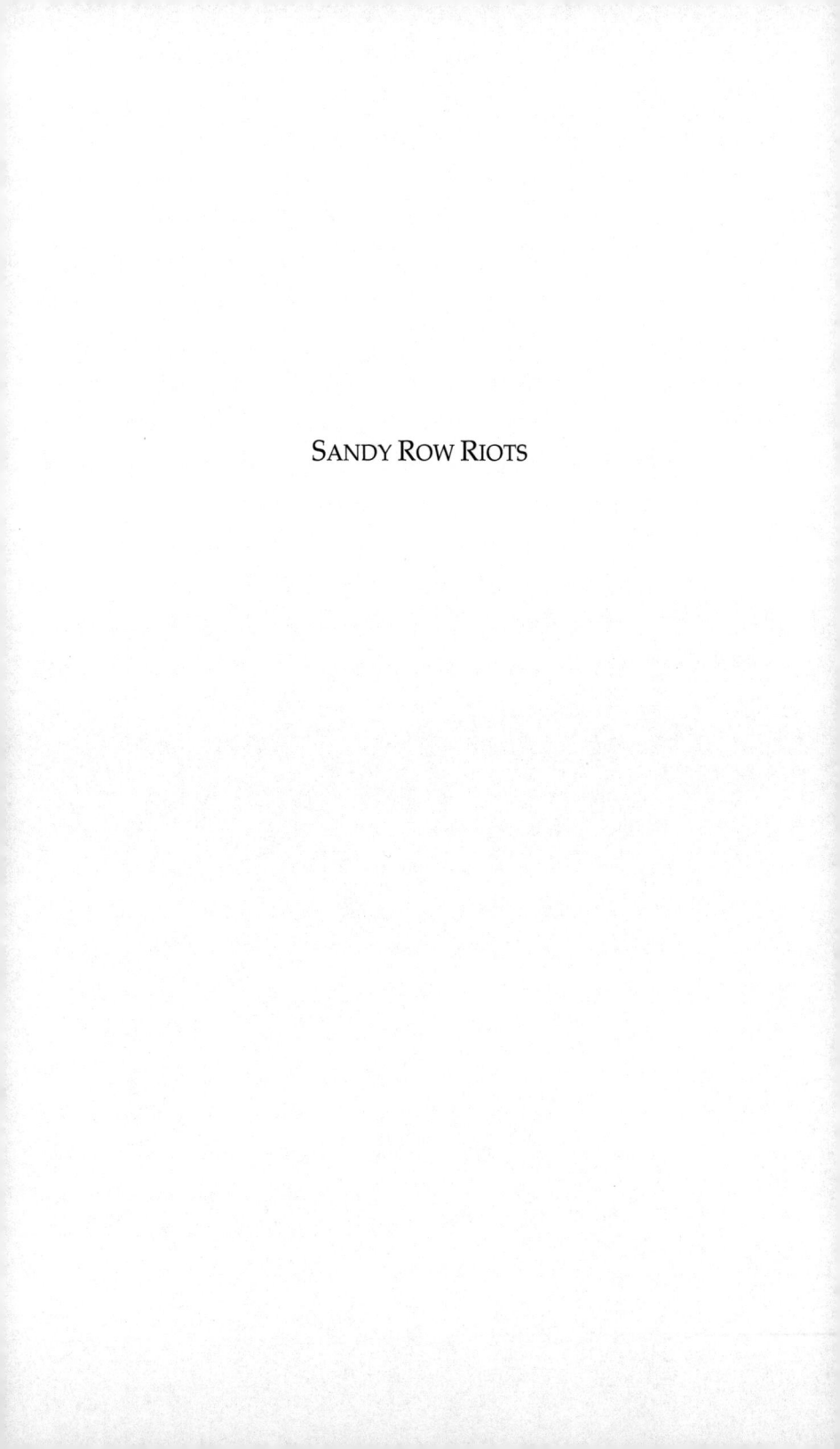

After Daniel McColgan's Murder

His body lies on the pad
under the ash, next to a blackthorn,
in the soft hollow of the devil's punchbowl.
(His dad says the devil only lurks in dark corners).
Ravens stalk his head
and tatted flowers creep round
the braeface of the caves
where United Irishmen stashed dreams.
A heart-bitter witness to his own eyes,
he named McColgan's killers.
'Way on to bed,' the peelers told him,
overbowled by the whiskey on his tongue,
and said to come again tomorrow.
The back end of day the killers took him
from his terraced home
and heeled him off from Freedom's Cap,
a living sacrifice to the truth.
They cowped him like the stone of kings,
the broken pelt hawked up
where harebells sleep
and whin bushes whisper
that the tongue is the giver
of life and death.

Orchardlands

Once an exile, I come from a long line of exiles.
My grandfather left his rain-pocked family farm,
fields rich with clabber,
apple trees clenched in bony witch's form
filigreed with frost
and sailed from Derry to New York
with a sovereign coin sewn into the lining of his coat.

He was an itinerant seller of glass,
hopping onto trains like a hobo,
even wittily marrying a girl named Glass
and slowly built an empire
stretching from Kansas to LA,
only to lose the lot in the Wall Street Crash
along with his younger brother who turfed himself
from a glass window, exiling his body to death.

My grandfather returned to Armagh
where my father dreamed the same dream
of bright, open lands
away from the crepuscular rainclouds, the ceaseless
tending to the apple, plum and pear,
the demands of a land that its natives
cursed when they were forced to leave.

At fifteen, my father ran away to sea
and became a lifelong exile,
seeing each docked ship fade
from the rear window of his taxi
as he happily sped away,
later ending his days in a wind-breached border town
between England and Scotland.

I left for the mainland myself at nineteen;
a strange term that, mainland,
like we were the minorland.
I taught my own tongue from Nancy to Athens,
moving from city to city
like they were carriage compartments,
a permanent suitcase strapped to my back,

a dreamcase, and when I ended my exile
I came home to my land of holy cloud-prismed light,
the people's humour as sharp as a blackthorn,
their faces open as apple blossom,
and here I'll stay, settled now,
with my sovereign of hope
still sewn into my coat.

Bukowski Blue

'I want to get you drunk,' he says
in the Japanese restaurant,
sipping on homemade sake
as rough as ethanol.
'Your hands are so soft,'
he says holding one,
and I laugh and tell him
it's strange that soft hands
can write such cruel things.
He eats his tempura fast,
faster than a wolf in a pack
– *tempura fugit* –
with a surprised expression,
raised eyebrows,
while I suck on my noodles, and he says,
'Imagine if your lips stayed
like that, all puckered in a kiss,'
and I think of his mouth
on my clitoris,
the softness of his tongue,
the hardness of his teeth.
And when he's eaten, he asks,
'What's the word for this?'
'What word?'
'The word between satisfied
and content.'
So I say there isn't one
while he blows
on his green tea
and I feel his breath
and I know he will enter me later
as I lie on my side
and suck and blow on my ear.

We pay up
and walk out into the street
to see the worn-out denim of the hills
and the red bricks fading
into a smokey penis-pink
and I wonder what the word is
between 'perfect' and 'gone forever'
before realising that
there is no right word for it –

no
words,
in fact,
at all.

The Smile Clinic

Now your breasts are plumped and primped
it's time to attend to the tartarland tragedy of your teeth.
Before your implant, the dentist runs her silver mirror
over every item in your toothcase like she's inspecting
a parade ground – incisors, veneers, canines, crowns,
premolars, molars, wisdom teeth, amalgams –
you have more mercury than a gold mine – all present
and correct save for one gaping gap in your gum.
'Let's numb you up,' she says, reclining you, slanting
the sun of the operator light into your eyes. A sharp pain,
then a slew of grapefruit bitterness runnels into your throat.
She warns you of the weirdness you're about to feel:
'Tap me if you need me to stop,' and screws
the metal into the gum, then it's bang
on your bone, the surreal battering
echoing in your brain – you feel like a defiled ossuary,
a fossil chiseled from some strange strata.
Eyes tight shut, you beseech yourself to relax,
mandible and maxilla prised apart to the max,
jaw so distended you could swallow her hammering
forearm whole in one voluptuous gulp.
Mercifully, she breaches your stone wall,
plants the post in triumph like a flagpole,
stitches you up and lets you rise, fractured,
unsteady on your feet, grunting a confused goodbye
as you totter past Tracey the receptionist
into the cold bite of the air, into the apricot light,
where you begin the slow alchemy back from bone to flesh
and, muscling your tongue against the bloody buttress
in your mouth, you know it'll all be worthwhile
when you smile.

The Wake at Turf Lodge

We drive up into the nape of the mountains,
close to where the Hatchet Field
is etched into the blood-ferned slopes,
through terraced streets where witches
and skeletons are flying from the porches
in a phalanx of Samhain nightmares.
Enter at your peril, says a sign.

The front door wide open, Seán greets us
in a voice as warm as hillside honey. 'Come on in.
We only got him home today.'
His da is in the coffin, the silk
drawn up to his waist like a chrysalis,
his fingers clasped in latticework,
unnaturally gapped like a mountain wall,
wrinkled like they've been in water.

His closed eyes are sunken and it seems odd
for him to be wearing his glasses.
A photo rests on the table,
an aide-memoire to his younger self
where his skin was a posy pink.
Mass cards are massed on the floor
around the coffin, open-winged,
an angelic white and gold.

In the kitchen there are forty shades of soup
and not a bun in sight
nor a drop of drink either
but a heady brew of black humour
from Seán who decants the tale of how
'My da dropped dead in the pub –
must have been the price of the pints.'

Back in the 'living room'
– a misnomer if ever there was one –
newcomers pay their respects,
two teenagers staring at each other,
ateing the leg off themselves with lust,
and as dusk settles over the mountains,
the moths, pale-winged, flutter in,
ash-like, offering up their dancing bodies
to the heart of the hall light.

Belfast

I was born in the east of the city
between Belmont and Dundela,
with the wind of the lough in my lungs,
the shudder of bombs in my bones,
the rust-red of bricks in my hair
and the strength of the cranes in my soul,
their yellow lighting up
the biblical greylands of Ballyhackamore.
My mother had a petrol-bomb temper
and kept me close to her
within the precincts of our apple-treed garden
as if heart-scared of losing me
to the mad dogs who scoped
the streets at night.
I sought freedom in the bookcase,
leafing through *Treasure Island*,
Seven Little Australians, sunny, havening retreats,
but all I could smell from their pages
was the damp of our moss-laden streets.
In those days the whisper of the rain on the leaves
was like the vestigial spittle of our prayers:
'Forgive us our trespasses as we forgive those who
trespass against us.' Only we didn't forgive
and the hate was scored into my brother and me
as deep as the Hatchet Field on Black Mountain.
We raced around like other kids
playing British Bulldog in Strandtown school
while bomb roars rippled through our garden,
singing our songs about Georgie Best and Elton John,
or John Elton as we called him to burst his stardust
and I'd be in wrinkles at my jokes,
fairly losing the run of myself
though, at times, Mum would turn pensive
and say, 'There'll be a quare lot of rain in the hills

for all that laughing,'
reminding me for my own good
of the dark that lay beyond the Belmont light.

The Wand

Rohan, the bodhrán maker, asked
what he could make for me
and I said, 'a wand', almost as a joke,
little thinking he'd really make one.
A month later he'd fashioned one
out of hazel, short and sinuous,
pale as driftwood, little oval eyes
where the twigs once grew,
a twine of green Irish wool wrapped
tight around the handle.

The pub, fumed with yeasty kegs,
blurred into a vague backdrop
as Rohan gave me the caveats:
'Never use your wand indoors but in wide open
spaces,' he said, 'away from any trees.'
I put the wand in a drawer, scared of Celtic
gods and sacred powers, until one stormy day
the cantor of the wind sung strong
and the leaves were flying from the trees
like pages out of a grimoire

and I brought my wand out into my street,
pointed it through the gap in the beeches
into the arching sky beyond and realised then
that I was the author of my own power
and I could get everything I desired on this earth
because it wasn't the wand I had feared
or any ancient lore of oak, ash or hazel;

all that I had feared was myself
and my own power.

Cregagh Glen in March

'Do you hear the trees sing?' you ask.
The air is full of the shrill voices of pines
above the guttural gurgles and stutters of the glen
as we slip and slide down the steep guttered path.

We reach out for the ghost of old handrails
long since sidled into the heart of the waterfall,
while the gale rages overhead, a sonic roar in the branches,
an aircraft aria, the song of the sycamores.

Storm-felled trees lie awkwardly, limbs twisted
like people shot in mid-flight
and one tree has raked out half the hillside with its roots,
the crocuses unearthed in bulging white globes.

The path now rises above the colloquy of whispering
willows and plunges down towards the ferned fallwater
where tines seem frozen in perpetuity
as time stops still and movement coalesces

and we watch without daring to breathe,
trying to capture the truth of the scene
as we would try to limn a snowflake when it falls,
a butterfly in flight,

an inchoate thought,
the soughing of the firs above,
and suddenly – yes – we see the water as it is:
a shoreline of silver threads glinting behind
a glaze of glass.

Heliophile

All her life my mother lapped at the sun,
sucked its honey up through a straw,
her arms outstretched like a hieratic worshipper,
chin tilted, eyes closed under its drowsing celestial power
and she would drift for hours on her sun lounger,
drenching her skin in Ambre Solaire,
tutting at my pallor, casting a withering
roll of her brown eyes at how my skin lobstered
and peeled in calamine calamity
while the sunlight coated her in an even golden glow.
To see her, you'd have thought our lawn
was the Côte d'Azur,
the sound of traffic, the whisper of the sea.

On the Twelfth she would stay there,
unmoved, looking at the insides of her orange eyelids
and when a bomb purred deep in the city
her lashes would tremble but never open.
Then, as the sun set, she would stand, snap her bikini
back over her buttocks
and slink loose-limbed into the kitchen
in voluptuous self-appreciation.

Sometimes she'd tell the story of her glory days:
how at twenty years old she holidayed in Italy
where the *regazzi* were fooled by her olive hues
into thinking she was Italian too –
Bella! Bella! went their cries
when she sashayed through the *piazza*.

But now, in her last months of lung cancer,
and on the best day of the year,
she hirples out to the garden,
scapula hunched, her wheezing breaths

in tune with the wind's rustle of the leaves.
I attend to her with cushions,
placing them on the wooden bench like some courtier
while she has her audience with the sun,
her shirt cuffs swamping her hands, white hat
wielding a swaddling shadow over her face
– mindful of the danger of the light on her chemo –
but how I long for her to feel the sun on her skin
one last time,
so what I do is stay with her,
roll up my sleeves,
exposing my white skin
to the naked glare
and take the rays on her behalf,
burning, scorching, reddening by the second,
immolating myself on the patio pyre,
making sure to tell her
how beautiful it feels.

An Aphorism on Divis Mountain

By the belly-bulge of a solid wall
we rest a second under the mountain,
pale brown and smooth as a cow's back,
before climbing up to the neolithic standing stones
limed white with lichen, their muddy tuile
a rusted iron ore. Dried grass is caught
on a barbed wire fence like oatmeal wool
on a loom. You belong here, breathing in the air
and deciphering the difference between the smoke
of kindling and turf. Slowly I can feel you
taking the boulders of my shattered heart
and, one by one, putting them together
in a dry stone wall to keep out the cold wind.
And from here we look back down onto the city
where the sunlight glitters from the cars;
constant stars lighting up, then disappearing.

Then Suddenly

Belfast is a heavy winter coat
that's seen better days,
whiskey-stained, trailing on the road
of salt and whirling sand,
blowing us away in the downdraft of a dream,
the snow a swarm of ice-cold insects,
slates on the roof frost-white and black
like a chess board. A succession of fag-burned days follow,
the fog merging with the marijuana fumes
from the old shipyard houses, reverberating
with a low TV hum that tells us Mariupol is burning
down to its bare bones, and I watch myself walk through
the architrave of a curved thornbush ...

Then suddenly
the buds are quivering candles in a breeze as soft
as your breath on mine in bed
and spring is pursed lips,
puckering up,
then bursting into fulsome smiles
as the lads swagger out
with fresh-shaved heads like catkins,
bums tight as unfolded blossoms.
And from the hillside the sun cuts through the heat haze
in the bowl of the city, lighting up
the white breeze blocks, making it
look like Rome or Athens, so much so
Belfast is blasted away
and I sigh to myself, 'Oh, Belfastia,'
while all around me fresh leaves are budding
from gnarled knuckles
bursting with the truth that youth
can spring from any age.

Ravenhill Bonefire

'The sun always shines on the Protestant people'
goes the saying on the Twelfth
– though it's often lashing down –
but as the sun dips its head on Lismore Street
women charge out with their child-filled chariots,
their throats torced in night-glo necklaces, while men
tumble out of pubs, fags in their gubs, and the DJ
drowns out the twilight starlings in their trees; just then
the tower stretches up like the spine of a wicker man,
and as the night turns dark as a blackthorn stick,
the fairy feet of the laser lights dance on the pallets
and the youth ignite them with their petrol bombs.
The foreign flag is the first to be devoured by flames
to tribal, ribald cheers: 'Keep 'er lit, lads!' shout the elders
whilst red embers in an orange cloud plume out above
the smoke and the black breath of a rival boney rises above
the rooftops and the land is lit up like a summer's day,
the lights flickering in the nearby windows as if
there are bright fires beating within all the houses
and the woodburn heart warms the bare faces of the crowd
who happily declare for another year,
'Sure the heat'd keep you going till Derry Day!'

Call of the Ancestors

As I hurry down London Road to Lismore Street
at near to midnight on the eleventh night
the air is taut with the sound of fissling static

and when I turn the corner
the bonfire is hissing and spitting
great forked tongues of flame.

There are cheers of fear from the crowd
as pallets topple perilously then fall
and the wonder grows, pollinates

as we look up to a spiraling helix of embers
in the July sky, party-popping into
a blizzard of bright orange flakes falling

down on us like scalding sleet from a black smoking sky,
and all around me, people peak their hands across their
eyes as they stare into the ferocious sun of it

with sempiternal pride
without even knowing that this is Lismore
from the Irish *Lios Mór* meaning great ringfort

nor knowing that history is destined to repeat itself
and that this grassy land once lumined another tribe.

Making the Most of the 1912 Suite

In Stormont Hotel we're upgraded
to the 1912 Suite which has a glistening
white bath and the obligatory photo
or two of the Titanic. I like to avoid the taint of tragedy
wherever I go but no matter. Down we go
to the bar with a view of the conference rooms where
we spot a guy in a suit scrolling through his phone
for women in swimsuits. No matter. We order
soup and wheaten bread but the bar staff forget about us.
It's kind of typical, we say, considering our government
doesn't do a hand's turn at Stormont either.

When we go back to our suite
you disappear into the room with the white bath
and when you come out again I note
that you're undressed. 'No, I've dressed for the evening,'
you correct me with a grin as we merge
and you unpeel my clothes like you're stripping
the petals from a flower. You rub my left nipple,
watching the slow rise of it, observing it intently
like bread rising in an oven and I feel
the thrust of you before my flesh waves from my buttocks,
to my stomach, to my breasts in one giant swathe.

Yes, I think you could say we joyfully degraded
the pristine surroundings of our upgrade.
And in this 1912 Suite on our white ocean liner of a bed
I grab once more at the life vest of your buoyant body
but the mattress is easing me down.
I feel my heart diving deep into yours, mirroring its sonar
beat and I'm sinking,
sinking
    s   ing
     ink

Hic Jacet
after Thomas Campbell

To live in hearts we leave behind
is not to die, says the poet,

but how long do the hearts who remember us
live on; seventy or eighty years at most?

To live in pages we leave behind
is not to die

and to live in the hearts of readers
who come after us is the only road to immortality

worth walking, and every poet knows it.

Axis Mundi

It's the tiny things that matter on our trip to Armagh,
the way you tug on my arm when I cross a busy road,
the way you lace up my walking boots tight,
the way you warm my hands in the hyperborean wind
but our minds don't meet and match
and back in the hotel here's the catch
– while I talk of the future, riven with striving,
you tell me you only live for the now.

Why does every time with you
feel like the first and the last?
The thirst and the gasp, the burst and the clasp.
In the graveyard we can't even find the past,
whispering 'sorry' when we step on the graves,
our boots slipping in the mud and the clay.

On our final morning at Navan Fort
the air is dizzy with the buzzard's call
and when we climb up to the mesocosm,
heaven and earth collide, past and present,
till we are suddenly blown off our axis,
the tines of light shining down on us
and all is limpidly clear why we're here and
why the world has sewn us together.

CUBERDON (OR THE IMMUTABILITY OF BELGIAN LOVE)
for Marc

It arrives with a Belgian postmark,
a poke of Ghent noses,
floral, perfumy and cloudy purple,
talcumed like Turkish Delight,
a gift fit for a seraglio.
Inside are amethysts of
crystallised sugar leading into
tonguable dark red jelly
and oozy innards buried deep within
like a perfectly formed blood clot
transfused straight from your heart.

Oceanus

It's still on my mind,
the seaside Airbnb
that couldn't contain the raw thrill
of our undress and touch
like we were holy salvage
or in the midst of a feeding frenzy
and how other lovers may have had the best of us
but you tried and foamed and lashed your body to mine
as the Irish Sea battered on the door.

And it's still on my mind,
the condom lying like a wet mermaid's purse,
our heart urchins pulsing,
of how we laughed
when we came to leave
and couldn't find your phone
until we found it washed up in the tide of sheets
and I felt the tow of you
as we swam up into the sun.

Madden's Bar, Castle Court

They're like mushrooms spreading, fanning out in
the damp, woody room,
pinky brown caps in the shade like beerheads sprouting,
their breath fugging the windows.
Across warped joints of ceiling planks the light spawns
ripples, the snug wood swallows harsh words into a hum.
Heat grows, crucibles, steams the room into a Palm House,
a girl branches her body over a boy and her lips bow
heavy as pink blossom
dousing, drowsing his face with honeydew,
but suddenly the fire exit is opened for the coolness
and fermenting rings plump up again, gills ruffling
and they slurp the scum off the bog in their glasses
and puffball their cheeks
before the spores fly around the room with the news
that the peelers say
it's time to close.

Sandy Row Riots

A long, hot summer is promised
in haw-red letters daubed
on the baked outer wall

of inner city rath and bawn.
Infurnaced people, copter-crazy,
entranced by gauzy wraiths

from flaming underbellies of engines
that catch like fireweed,
come from the East and Tiger's Bay.

Fireworks scythe the tarmac,
glowflies bumping over peaty waters.
'They keep your feet warm!' goes the crack.

Saracens are lured into the crucible
of cul-de-sacs and, bombed,
reverse with rolling wakes of fire.

Rubble-cairns tipped from crates
are fed upon like bread for crows
and the leaders, snooded and scarfed

from mountain winds, orchestrate,
raking out old, dead fires for folk
on the brink of ceasefire suicide

like drovers herding over gullies
where each year the heather is lit and burnt
so that it can live once more.

Sham Supermarket, Sandy Row

The English half of the signage
is burnt away to nothing; only the Arabic
survives. Baby aubergines lie
by the smashed frontage, bunches
of withered mint, blackened lemons,
ashen avocados in the windowless remains.

Outside Syrian men are gathering
under the watchful eye of smokers loitering
in the pub doorway across the road.
'I'm not scared,' one man is telling
a journalist, though his face says
otherwise, 'but three years I worked here.'

The shutter is hanging at half-mast as you
lower your head and step onto the wet
mulch of sunflower seeds, roasted corn
and spices, an exotic bogland,
a Persian carpet with pools in the aisles
rippling under a dark dripping ceiling.

Charred pistachios are piled
on the flame-leathered skin of the counter
beneath white plastic stalactites.
You crunch through sugared almonds
while gloved men salvage what they can
from the scorched shelves: warped bottles
of yellow oil, fire-darkened olive jars,
melted cribs of toasted sesame.

You're just leaving when a voice
shouts out behind you, 'Wait!' The owner,
Bashir, runs after you and presses
into your palm a gift saved from the fire,

a cube of malban, a little piece of heaven
for your tongue, and rising through
the stale aftermath of the air,
a hint of fragrance and belonging.

The Pint

My pal's outgoing,
will sit in any company,
can come across cold
this tabletop martyr, this pub idol
but, strong-headed at first,
the more you speak to him
the clearer his views become.
He welcomes the friendly clasp of hands
and opens the mind full-tilt,
brings the pub out of Republican,
the order from the Orangemen.
To him party politics
means 'who gets off with who?'
So, one for the road
that's free of flags and colours
because my pal is the best offer yet
to be laid on the table.

Choosing the Unbeaten Path

The August morning after you told me
you'd met another woman
who'd look after you
and I said I understood
as I could barely look after myself
we drove up to Black Mountain,

our eyes following the sun patches
racing along the summit.
There was a wind up there
to make our heads light,
the hollow pipes of the gates fluting
while ghostly voices disputed.

We took the Ridge Path
over the slabbed granite stones
through the wild sucking bog
and grassland stippled
with red and white clover
where you picked me a shamrock,

a trefoil to twirl in my fingers,
then pointed to the tiny Irish orchids
hiding shyly behind the butter daisies.

At the ridge we stopped at a huge boulder
cratered with wind-quivered water
and I dipped my hand in it like it was
a holy font while you looked out
lost in your own private dreams
to the fabulated blue of the Mournes
floating in the mist over the horizon.

On the way back, we diverged further.
I started to stray off the paved path
to where the heather was soft to the sole
and the marsh yielded underfoot
and bog cotton swished off my calves
making me plunge wildly into the bulrushes
up to my thighs as I crushed the orchids
and sent a nesting swallow skittering up in alarm

while you watched on indulgently, all the time
stepping on the centre of each stone,
knowing exactly where you were going,
never deviating.

The Peacebroker

'Come here with your cameras.
Go on, shoot. We've shot in our time.'
The press queue up like kids at an ice-cream van,
the statesman sweats under his makeup
but it doesn't show.
The son of a gun is now a family man
dripping with charm,
hands dripping with blood,
trading in the combats for a suit
seems astute these days.
There's a metallic glint in his eye,
a threat that makes orphans cry,
but while demagogues roar like the ocean
he is gently spoken,
well-versed, immersed in his task.
He hands over the nettle
he wants others to grasp.
Now a people's politician
he's hurt by their suspicion
but every now and then
he forgets to pretend.
'We love peace,' he avows, 'we're looking to the future.
But the past, it hasn't gone away, you know.'
The man with a mission
wants no less than submission,
his finger on ignition.

A Belfast Summer

There is a grey hangover of a sky
drunk from a debauched summer
sweating out beads of warm rain.
Moss is draping the roofs
and weeds are sprouting with Dionysian flair,
roses unfurling like they have notions of themselves,
dreaming of a tropical ravine.

Leaving the house is like walking
into a launderette, the sky the pale rumpled grey
of a white duvet cover
washed with the darks by mistake.
The streets are silent, everyone languishing indoors
exhausted from the oppressive stillness.

I lie in bed with you, looking out
at the rented dinginess of the clouds
and feeling the cool pool of your breath
on the hot pillowed nape of my neck.

Noah Donohoe

The glen runs swift from the steeps of Cave Hill
down to the echoes under the rusted iron grill,
rounding corners where the water gulps and slabbers
against the wet walls, the body bobbing
of the boy whose name floats to the tongue every day,
circling out across the city.

The colloguing willows swish their heads and waggle
their crooked fingers at the nearby terraced houses,
remembering the boy on the bike on that hot sunny day,
the tread of his wheels on the melting camber
spinning away from the Shore Road to explore
side streets smouldering from an old burnt-out conflict,
cycling for his life with his shirt ripped off his back,
fleeing the drunken afternoon mob
till he dropped his bike and ran for his life.

The glen gulders the names of the killers
who were protected by the peelers,
or so they say, but can you ever truly
trust the whispered beats of the tribal drums?
In the storm drain the water washes over his body,
erasing the bruises in its embalming sluice,
hiding the evidence, rinsing away the crimes,
cleansing the blood until all that is left
is a symphony of urban rhymes.

The Alice Kyteler Girl Gang

The Halloween sliced moon grins orange
above the streetlights and our hearts grow as fat
as pumpkins to hear the cracks and booms
of the dead exploding from their coffins, tombstones
crashing to the mud through the blood-veiled ferns.
We lock ourselves in our rooms, break our broomsticks
over the backs of the licking incubi, then fly
into the inky sky, swooping down to feast on passersby,
the firework flowers and fountainheads
blooming and bursting in a thud of sparkling buds,
disappearing as if by midnight magic
into one last cool puff of smoke.

On the Seabed

Before we go to the cool white bed in our hotel room
you and I decide to go wild in the Japanese restaurant
and share a white platter of sashimi, slivers of pink, raw
meat that we slice and rip in half: fuchsia-coloured squid,
slippery scallop, the fleshy red of tuna –
'Here, have some nipple,' you joke of a surf clam –
all resting under a Mount Fuji of wasabi and ginger
followed by a coral bed of crispy white tempura,
a glorious picture for the eyes that pitches
our delicate Irish stomachs into a gurgling Fukushima
meltdown. 'Is that my stomach or yours?'
you ask with widened eyes
as we grip onto our yonomis full of bilious yellow tea
and let the sashimi slither through our chopsticks
and decide to stick to the sticky rice to save ourselves.
We pay the bill quickly before our love-making plans
hit ruination and, as we leave our table,
the soft-shell crabs wave their arms at us
and seem to point us in the direction
of the nearest chippy; but all I can think of
is the kisses that will come from your pink lips
fuchsia lips
blood-red lips.

On Waiting for a Better Day

On a spirited November day
we head up to Knockagh Monument
basalt-black on the brow of the hill
and ascend the mazy hairpin lanes into
the blousy, drizzling clouds. Up there
poppy wreaths have been heeled into the fields
and we look down onto Carrickfergus Bay
as misty white as a condensated mirror
and you promise we'll return on a better day.

But I couldn't give a fuck if we do or don't
for this is the place with the cloud on the hill,
the sea on the shore, the castle on the coast,
the monument on the mound
that makes my heart slow
and the stress rill from my veins
for you are the wide-open space
that brings out my deepest thoughts,
your mood is my weather,
and there will never be a better day than this.

L'Oreille en Rose

We all ate raclette on Colette's birthday night
with great plates bursting with layers of pink prosciutto
and then we swayed in our chairs as Piaf soared
and cut through the laughter with her quivering *cri de
coeur*. I gave Colette a birthday card that wished her a year
of dirty pleasures and she smiled and gave me a drunken
kiss from her champagne-doused lips that missed
my cheek and collided sublimely with my ear, and for
the sweetest second my helical folds held her warm
wetness like a corolla of rose petals
awakening to the dew in the dawn sun.

Christmas Beach Party

At Holywood beach at Christmas
the sea is smooth with lanes of freshwater

coursing through the ocean camber
under a calm grey sky streaked with eastern blue

while the yellow cranes in Belfast Harbour mimic
the crook-necked gulls feeding on the shoreline

and the panorama wheels from the white mansions
on Cave Hill all the way to the pastel seafronts of Larne.

Alone I walk to the banks of shingled sea belt
washed up on the sand and the fronds of oarweed

that are like streamers ripped down
during a wild ocean party along with garlands

of samphire, pine cones and clams, a tangle of festive lights
in the periwinkles shining from the acid kelp.

The tide plays with me, trying to bubble up
and soak my feet in a sudden surge –

a lone seal, head bobbing as she paddles towards me,
disappears into the depths for her yuletide dinner.

A tinselly light catches the pebbles,
the whelk eggs as delicate as a paper decoration

and in a champagne moment I step on the bladderwrack
which pops and sprays its sea foam into the air

and the geese who winter here
blow their party horns
and all nature is with me.

An Ode to Dangerous Women

On a warm sun-sinking evening in Tel Aviv
I'm stopped at border control by a gimlet-eyed guard,
Slavic-featured, flame-haired, tight-lipped,
and told I cannot enter because of 'national security'.

I'm ushered by police into a van with a Canadian
called Mariam Bhabha and whisked through miles
of airport land of scruffy dead-leafed palms and shuttered
huts with sunken roofs full of fronds lying out like herbs
drying on a rack. Electric cables dangle rootless
from the walls, refuse caught in the teeth of fences,
scarlet sports cars sitting in open garages.

At the detention centre the policemen fire out acronyms,
wanting us to confess our illicit membership;
they turf our luggage out onto a table and after
a long drawn-out search make us repack
five times in total, lingering on their little
power trip, telling us, 'You are dangerous women.
We have peace here. Haven't you heard of the Oslo
Accord?'

At last they give us bed sheets and metal jugs of water
and take us to our cell. The bunks are full, so we have to lie
on rubber mattresses next to the doorless toilet,
the light squinting into our eyes until just before dawn
when the Lithuanians leave and the morning mauve
lightens the meshed frosted glass of our window.

A Hispanic woman keeps rapping on the door
with her ringed fingers and yelling, 'Embassade'
like a butterfly beating its body on a pane
but through the tiny glass square uniformed figures
zip past ignoring us until the next flight leaves

and, one by one, they all depart, including Mariam,
the sun squeezing its freshly-pressed lemon light
into the cell and I can't sleep a wink
still stunned that I am a threat to a nation
and excited by it too, my pulse singing a paean
to rebellion.

Willowfield Parade

In August little puffs of seeds are augustly
floating in the wind from the aspen trees
like bubbles blown by a playful child
when, out of nowhere, drums and flutes break
the dreamy silence, bursting through alleys
and entries, circling through the cul-de-sacs.

On Willowfield Parade a crowd is waiting
for the returning heroes. The bass drummer,
harnessed into his white shoulder straps,
ploughs on, blinkered, pucely-sweating,
lamming the goat skin, while
a small boy with *Protestant Prince*
on his t-shirt covers his ears and wails.
The fluters follow, swagger-hipped
and purse-lipped, as the drum major cries,
'Legs Up!', the seedheads sighing by,
coyly spinning in the breeze.

Outside the Cosy Bar the colour party
turns to face the band for
God Save the Queen. 'Hip hip hooray,'
they cheer, ending with a clash of cymbals
and the sky slowly waves its peach-crepe clouds
while the band fall out, spent,
limping with their bottles of buckie
back to their bus, the aspen seeds
swaying drunkenly at their feet.

The Courtship

My grandfather at twenty moved to digs in Dromore
at a farm called 'The Wood'
nestled in the dell of a hazel-treed hillock.

There were three daughters; the eldest was Winnie,
shy and skittish-eyed before him and the harvest
farmhands she helped to feed.

That August she'd sunbathe out of sight on the stable roof
but on his way back from working at the Ulster Bank
he'd catch a glimpse of her limbs pearled in the sun.

In September he returned to his room unwell,
shivering, his tonsils a raspberry red and by the next day
a rash had stained his torso and his tongue.

The doctor came, pinched his beard and shook his head,
saying it was scarlet fever and up to God's grace
if the lad saw out the week.

Winnie crept into his room with compresses
and wet white cloths, waving them in surrender,
turning her back on her mother's pleas to take care.

She sat by my grandfather's bed for days, soothing
the autumn fires in him and the rose-hip red in his organs,
beakering drops of well water between his lips.

One day he awoke to feel a cool breath on his cheek;
the heat stanched out of him, pillow-pale,
he watched Winnie open the drapes to let in the sun.

Six months later, in the spring of 1930, they married.

White Nights

'You'll be the death of me,' he says as I
make him run across a car-streaked road.
It's so cold outside our breaths turn
the air white and it's joyous like we're
spray-painting the world with our existence.

'Look, our light's still on,' he says,
pointing up to our Europa Hotel room
and I reply that it must be the waiter
bringing us our champagne and strawberries –
with heavy irony, of course.

Up in our room I go for a shower
and he joins me, the hot steam rising
whitely and it's like our very bodies
are smoking with desire. On our bed
he pulls me onto his lap

and places his hand on my chest
and places my hand on his chest,
right on his heart. As he breathes in
he tells me to breathe out, to make me feel
the inner pulse of him, and the breath,
the breath, the breath.

After Intimacy

After intimacy he can't quite bring himself
to leave me alone. 'Can I take this away with me?'
he asks of my nipple, twirling it between his fingers.
He shows me the book he's reading, *In Praise of Women*,
like he's proving what a great guy he is.

After intimacy he makes me milky tea
while he makes black coffee for himself,
narrowing his eyes at its heat like he's a seer,
staring out to the orange December sun
that sinks in the pearly glow of cloud
like a low table light from some
louche burlesque nightclub.

After intimacy he tells me about the swallow
who nests on the beam of his shed and skims
through his hair and he shows me a photo
of a robin sitting on the wheel of his car
as if asking him to never leave home again
and it makes me feel better about leaving.

After intimacy I stroke his peach-short hair
and get dressed while he watches me,
still seeing the palimpsest of my nakedness
underneath. 'Oh, you're leaving me,'
he exclaims in some sort of sad surprise
even though he must know that a love like ours
only shines bright on the pain of parting.

Proverbs for all Writers

A rejection a day
keeps the ego away.
A word in time
saves nine.
Axioms speak louder
than words.

HALF-DEAD POETS SOCIETY
after Dorothy Parker

I knew I'd never reach old age
as my spirit's too wild for my bodily cage.
My sense of immortality was always too strong
so I lit my own inner petrol bomb,
destroyed my liver from drinking long
and wrecked my lungs from smoking bongs.

An Illumination in Bittles Bar

I take my Belgian lover the circuitous route
along the damp-circled flagstones of Joy's Entry
following a bright moon bisected by a line of cloud.
'What's circuitous?' he asks and I tell him it's
the long way, the roundaboutery, and sometimes
it's hard how we lose each other in language,
how he can't see the dandering ways of my city.
Inside Bittles, its interior red as a heart,
we notice how the rare whiskey bottles
behind the bar are lit up like sculptures and
we laugh at the paintings of Paisley and Wilde.
The barwoman pours him a Guinness and we watch
as the brown whirls into a pale sandstorm
settling in the glass in one slow swirl to black
that leaves us in mutual awe of Irish magic –
I looking at him, him looking at me – taking
a shortcut to understanding; no words needed.

It's the Animal in Me, Baby

Half the night we sit up talking
about the days we spent as
housemates
in that shabby house in Larkstone
Street and how one night, a year
after the house was sold, you went back,
drunk as a punk, and rapped on the door,
shouting out my name, cause
you always were a wild one.
You still are with your defiant
quiff, that rip in your jeans
like you want to rip the world,
rip the clothes off women,
and your wider-than-wide-open
eyes always looking for trouble.
I keep the fun going by plying
you with spiced berry gin till your
eyes turn the same shade of pink.

The next morning the sun's peering in
under the blinds like a child's torch
under a duvet when I wake up
beside you in bed.
You ask, 'Are you feeling animal?'
and you grin, explaining how all animals
have sex in the morning –
and I'm not sure you're right
but David Attenborough isn't around
to ask so I let you move onto me
and bounce me hard and high,
launching me with your haunches,
belting me with your pelt,
taking sharp fast intakes of breath
as if my skin is too painful

or hot for you and, oh, it's glorious,
this final quivering shake of you,
this afterquake inside of you.

Afterwards we go out for breakfast
in a fried-soda-bread caff,
the grease fogging the window,
but we can still see the mountains
crowned by moss, dark and then
lightening by turns in the sun
to a bright voltaic green
like a flickering neon sign
and you smile at me
but I can still hear your growl
deep within.

December

The first frost is the marriage of winter and earth,
a sieved powdering on the pavement and
candified leaves; puddles holding white bubbles
beneath their lacy panes like tiny balloons.

The elms in Ormeau Park are happed-up
wedding-goers in coats of lichen and ivy,
surrounded by a confetti of glistening sea salt.
The sun is moon-white in the mist –

oh, and the calcite white of the sky,
the mini ice sculptures, the crystalline tears of joy
and the coldness rosing the skin
against the flawless linen of the bridal bed.

But by night winter slips into her sparkling
black sequins, inviting us in to her velvet party,
wrongfooting us, tripping us up with a teasing smile,
making us fall helplessly into her arms.

Art

If you can do one thing before you die
go to Ormeau Park on a winter's dawn
to watch how the sun in the east looks out
at the dark canvas of the mountains
and paints its first bold brushstroke
of yellow ochre on Divis heath, moving
down to the burnt reds of bracken
and then alighting on the tallest buildings,
anointing the windows of the City Hospital
one by one with gold. Lowering still
the sun ignites the tree tops and inflames
the fairy lights of vermilion buds
encased in their flickering ice-blown bulbs.
After the first blaze of colour has subsided
there is one last thing to do before you go:
Look back east at the brush of bare brown branch
tipped with orange and marvel at how it blends
with the white and dove grey of cloud
to bring out the subtler tones of day,
though the heart still revels in the early riot.

Eternity in a Glass

What a night in Madden's! The clock
on the wall where the time never changes,
the pints multiplying in the columned mirrors,
the lit bar shining in the darkness
like a giant burner in a wooden hut.
There are more fiddle players than punters
and their heels crack against the floor
till our baluster chairs are jumping
in a mad kind of beerdance Riverdance.
Great shushes rise up and silence falls
for a warbling *sean-nós* singer to wail
his way through an anti-Brit lament
but our tongues are warmed on the cold beer,
great peaty glasses topped with an oatmeal foam
and we laugh at a man whose upper lip
is frothed by a beerhead moustache while
the streetlights shine through the clear Celtic
script on the frosted windows, casting
its insignia onto our chests and faces
and the most wondrous trick of all is that
the clock on the wall still says twenty to eight.

Tempus

Two days after my dad's death
from a stroke I return to the Wansbeck
to collect his watch.
In the hospital driveway I spot
a blackberry bush tumbling over a fence,
bursting with the fattest berries
full of blossomy styles in the briars,
black knotted clots bleeding crimson
into the tiny scores on my fingers
and I remember how my father
used to forage for cherries and elderflower
in the summer at Chain Bridge, and
in the autumn he'd head to Norham Castle,
his huge country hands twisting the cap
off a field mushroom, the white fleshy neck
yielding to his fingertips, its black gills
quivering like pages in the wind,
nature bowing to him, the scion of a farmer.

Years earlier were the long
brambling afternoons in Dundrum where
he took me to pick blackberries
on Moneylane Road
and I'm foraging
in the past for more bright fruits
that will spill forth their stories: a single rose hip,
a haw, even a bitter crab apple drips
its intoxicating cider onto the tip of my tongue.
In the hospital I say goodbye to the nurse;
my dad's watch weighs heavy in my hand
but time itself is lifting and I now know
I'll spend many fruitful hours with him
over the following days.

Westward Unbound

Chilling on my bed in Belfast
I listen to a westerly rattling the doors,
singing to Aeolus in the chimney pots,
insinuating itself with elverine guile
through the blue slates of the roof
and I'm thinking that a writer is a type
of seafarer, wandering from voyage
to voyage, steadily pulling on the bireme oars
to propel a story across
the blank oceanic straights of a page.

Neuroendocrine cancer, one of the
most aggressive lung cancers, was the diagnosis.
I thought my father might live a year but at the end of
August he had called me from Berwick in a panic,
in a wheezy, halting, tumbledown voice
retreating into his chest, telling me
he could no longer breathe.

And it was the end of August
if I didn't say so before
the end of ...
the end ...
the ...

Just before I caught my flight
to Edinburgh the respiratory consultant
phoned me from the Wansbeck.
Is he about to die? I asked and she hesitated,
as someone used to weighing up
her words, more like a lawyer
than a doctor, and she said, no, not in my opinion.
Maybe three or four weeks at most.
Three or four.

Finite. Those French films I used to watch
ended in *fin*.

My father's semi-detached which
had been lonely since Mum had died
and now lonelier still, seemed vast
like a cruise liner full of decks
and I kept roaming the rooms till late,
walking through the doorways before
wondering why I was there, liminal,
neither here nor there as Heaney said,
not knowing what to do with myself,
taking the wind-dried washing my father had left
in the basket on the kitchen table
and putting it in the chest of drawers
even though I knew he'd never
wear those clothes again.

In the hospital Dad was smiling,
sitting up in his chair, the newspaper next to him,
a news addict to the death – 'to the death',
now there was a phrase.
He was vague, his glasses were lost and
when I read him the headlines, they could have
come from another planet or a sailor's moon
for all they pertained to him.
Now take it canny when the consultant comes,
he warned me, and when she told us
I'm afraid it's bad news, he burst into tears
though he was never a crier in life; I never saw
him cry until a few discreet tears at
Mum's funeral. Fifty long years it took
till my father opened up to me.

And at this point, time slowed ...
slowed ...
The holy trinity of time on a clockface,
seconds, minutes, hours
were moving underwater.

My father was a master mariner
and every night of his life at sea
he would do the rounds of the ship.
That night in the house I couldn't sleep
for thinking of him wandering, unmoored,
in that hot, stifling ward, a little bemused,
searching for air for his beleaguered lungs.
Every evening in Berwick, religiously,
he would walk the roads, the Elizabethan walls,
keeping leeward out of the wind; he knew
every lick of that North Sea breeze from the Arctic
to the fjords and the westerly softness
weaving through the valleyed heather-saddled hills.

Oh, Dad, after Mum died you were listless,
missing her endearments,
lacking the ritual of hiding your cigarettes
from her, of waiting to hear her voice
shout down from the bedroom to call time
on your nightcap in the kitchen –
'Two sheets to the wind' you used to call
it if someone drank too much.
You, the inveterate dreamer, pulling my leg once
that you'd won big on the lottery
when you'd only won ten pounds
and I'd inherited your addiction to the hilt,
playing the literary lotto, the writing roulette
every single day of my life.

Circumstances will arise when some of the following
information will be of use:
James H. Jenkinson 1937–201?
(I laughed at the ever-optimistic question mark).
Phone Charles Mace Undertakers.
Phone Sanderson, McCreath & Edney to sell the house.
Go to the Royal Bank of Scotland and ask for my bond ...
These were the instructions waiting for me on the dining
table because you knew I was remiss when it came
to the practicalities of life.

The next day at the Wansbeck he was asleep.
I thought it strange how his left fist was clenched
like he was squeezing a thunderbolt.
The consultant arrived and told me
he had had an event during the night:
an event,
a show,
a performance,
a book launch,
what a euphemism 'an event' was for a stroke.
Strokes were common, she said, during
the end stage of cancer
and all bets were off.
How long has he got left, I asked,
and she said it all depends on him,
how long he wants to stay around.
A day or a week, who knows.

He tried to talk to me, addle-tongued, indistinct –
a recognition of futility in his eyes before he closed them.
I told him it was ok and I'd be there until the end
but all I could think of was
I didn't have any spare underwear with me.

I sat with him beside his white-sheeted bed
while he floated as on a broken piece of ice field,
moving into channels, feeling the breeze
currenting from the open window,
gliding past sea-smoothed archipelagos,
Pytheas heading ever more deeply into Hyperborea.
The draught was cold on my back but I didn't close it
as a sailor needs the wind as a writer needs a story.

Death is overrated.
Death is overrated, the consultant said to me matter-of-factly. It is just one moment and it could happen when you are in the cafeteria or popped out for one second. She was trying to explain to me that, as I was on my own, I should feel free to leave Dad's room without guilt.

I went and sat under the pergola in Tear Drop Garden
to pray for Dad's release. There was no sun
or moon in that dark orphanless sky.
I went to the tiny chapel to pray
he wouldn't live another day.
When I went back his breathing was ever more stertorous,
him writhing, unanchored, his body still strong,
locked in combat with his mind.
The thing you find with these tough old birds is
they never want to give up, the nurse said to me
as she injected him with morphine.
I asked her not to give him too much
so that he'd leave me on his own terms, at his own time.
It felt like the one thing I could do for him,
to let him decide,
let him be the executor of his own fate.

The following day, his breath was perceptibly shallower,
feathery, crestless. I read aloud from the paper
as the sun centimetred through the window across his bed,
the left jamb a gnomon. A gnomic gnomon
because I knew it meant more than the hours
were passing. Dad's cousin Eileen came for an hour –
bringing some newly-bought knickers, hooray!
We sat talking about our family, our history, our legends
and suddenly she said, look, your father has his hand up.
He wants us to hold it. She held it a while
and, when she left, I held it a short time
till it moved limply away and I couldn't help
feeling offended as if he didn't love me enough
– for there were times in my life
we'd had a distance between us,
 a legacy of long seatrips,
a marination of grievance
– because even though it is a father's death
we make it all about us and the hurt resurfaces
in the last hours even as the love swells ...

In the night the porter brought in my folding bed,
I told my dad I loved him and I'd be beside him all night
long and I drifted beside him on flotillas of thought,
my little tug boat pulling his great battling warship along.
I suddenly woke up sensing some huge absence.
His breathing had stopped and I jumped up in the dimlit
room to switch the lamp on. His mouth was still a little
open, a tiny gossamer skein of saliva tendriling from his
top lip, the chest quite still, his skin comfortingly warm.
So this was death. I ran to the desk to get the nurse.
So this was it. I didn't think this was overrated; it was
momentous. From my spirited father lying next to me
to death, animate to inanimate, a transubstantiation

in reverse. I kept reassuring him of what a great dad he'd
been, mindful of any lingering sentience as I packed his
bag, even comically taking his false teeth from his bedside
table though what I thought I wanted with them I didn't
know.

Waiting on my taxi outside, I cried, huge plangent bawls
to the heavens fit to echo through all the years I'd be
without him.

And now I voyage round these words
and maybe I want to smash the seas,
set a storm to end all storms through the oceans,
like Poseidon did to Odysseus, at the thought
that James Harding Jenkinson is no more,
dead, *FIN enfin*, retired from human service,
beached on the sinking sandbank of memory
but I'll keep travelling, hoisting the white sails,
charting new channels, naming them after him,
taking the ups and downs, the floods and the ebbs,
spring tides and neap tides,
starboard and portside,
prow to stern,
mizzen to main,
guided by old moons and new moons,
the spinning wheelhouse of the sun.
Keeping moving.

A Prayer in Kharkiv

It's the pull of nature
as the train rolls slowly
towards Kharkiv as if it
doesn't want to bring me there.
It's the pull of nature
in the fields of sunflowers
with their heads hacked off,
decaying like bodies
without body bags
that lie in other fields.

In Kharkiv Putin's face adorns
a poster with fangs of blood
like a B-movie villain.
And it's the pull of nature
propelling me to Gorky Park
as soldiers in cars camouflaged
with fir boughs drive along
streets so vast
the sky seems even vaster
and the silence is even
louder than the ever-present sirens.

And it's the pull of nature
as I look up through the torn clouds,
my shoulders crouching at first
in the fear of aerial assault
from drones and rockets,
before seeing the blue above
and the tremulous rays of yellow sun
that tell me to walk on undaunted
for heading our way, thank God,
is a weather front,
and not a battlefront.

Cailleach

After the deepfreeze of the night I totter out
onto the granular frost that cracks like popping candy.
The cliffs of Cave Hill are fissured under a fir of cloud,
the round cheeks of snow on the mountains pinked
into life by the rising sun. In my street a woman
is scraping an Inuit fishing hole on her windscreen
while her neighbour throws a bucket of boiling water
over her doorstep, watching the geysering steam
of an Icelandic *hver*. The sun wheedles its way through
the byways, a prankster loosening ice-floes in the puddles,
inching its slippery toes across the earth. At one point
I breathe in an eviscerating freshness so shocking it jolts
my lungs alive. Air such as this I never breathed before
and wow – it's like my first ever breath as a baby.

Wintering It Out

In January my friends and I talk of how
to get through the bewilderingly dark months:
Gwenn goes into her garden to ground herself
and plunges her hands into the black crumbling earth

that feels so different from the summer soil, but even so,
gives her hope; Seán says that nights in the company
of friends like us is the answer, raising his glass
of red wine as bright as his bloodstream on high.

And I? All I ask for is someone who marvels
at my body in the winter light, touching my skin like
they are touching a work of art, touching me
like I'm summer.

WALK, INTERRUPTED

I was twenty on a summer's day in Durham
when I took a shortcut through the fields.
It was a grass track bordered by bushes
on each side, full of pendulous giant leaves,

flowers throwing back their heads to face the sun
to be sexed and frottaged noisily by bees.
I walked alone, thinking nothing of it, having grown up
reading how Emily Brontë freely roamed the moors.

A young blond guy, handsome, rode on a motorbike
towards me, tossed me a smile, and as I stepped aside,
I smiled in return. I walked on, but heard the bike's purr
slow, turn, loudening, and he roared back past me,

shouting, jeans unzipped, penis swollen in his hand.
I panicked, the buzz of his bike in my ears
louder and louder, and he shuttled back towards me,
cheering himself on like a wild beast, warped with joy.

I looked away and started to run, my heart
shunting in an arc out of my body, praying
he wouldn't skid to a halt. Again, he passed me
but I could see the end of the track open up

into rugby fields, and on and on I ran until
the sound of his revs had exited the earth and students
were milling. All around me nature was outraged,
bees buzzing in crazy zigzags, jackdaws wheeling and

screaming, lacerating the sky with their flick knife wings,
banks of hemlock stamping and shaking their musk
or at least I thought so – perhaps they fell silent like me.

At the sports centre, I told my friends what had happened and they told me I was wrong to have taken the shortcut. I guessed they'd never read about Emily Brontë.

Blood Queen

When my periods stopped I didn't miss them at all. But sometimes, just sometimes, I think of how I used to pull out my tampon, cup my left hand and let the waiting blood pour into my palm which I would hoist up in front of me and say, 'Is this blood which I see before me?' It was my Lady Macbeth, Lady Macdeath, Lady Blackdeath moment and I milked it to the max like any self-respecting drama queen. I loved how the blood would trickle through the webbing of my fingers and I'd revolve my hand till the red ran round like a wedding band. And I loved when the blood came thick with a clot like a microwaved blackberry as if I'd wallowed in the vascular depths of an enemy, a murderer I, sending others to die, and I'd lick the divine effusion, my bloody flood, my ichor liquor, and I'd relish its base metallic taste, for the most beauteous moments of life are when it looks like death. So yes, overall, there are times I miss my period.

Nonconformist

The dawn comes, smoking rings of raincloud across
the glories of bright pink strata, making the spire
of St Anthony's turn a solid black
and birds fly out of the windchime branches
soaring like commuters into town.
But one sole raven stays on the tip of the Celtic cross,
its tail convulsing as it gauges the air,
me standing there perched on my doorstep,
the belfry of my chest ringing out
as the raven swoops, swept up in the laterals,
dropping on the sudden wind-lull,
imagining itself hurtling to the ground, angling,
vertiginous, and I follow it with my eyes,
my soul-twin, dicing with death,
writing the dream of the sky
with its wings.

BEING SAVED AT WHITEROCK
for Gemma

My street is a swirling fosse of cries,
barks and alarms, awash with overfilled skips.
Every evening I walk home past the Catholic
Jesus so muscled he seems to have a six-pack and
past the needy teen who haunts the off licence,
asking me to buy him a can of Dragon Soop.
Later I keep wakening in the steep trenches
of the night, troubles exploding in my chest,
waiting, aching in my own shadowy Erebos
for the inner-city dawn.

One morning you call at my house by chance
and spirit me away through wintergreen acres
and purple cabbage fields, past Lisbane and Killinchy
to a different land where
the sun bounces blindingly off the sea.
There the soft crepitation of the dried black seaweed
carpets my feet next to the lapping lulling waves
and the gentle tide slows my heart like sleep,
pulling the flotsam and jetsam of cares
from my fingertips
and, finally,
I am saved.

A Playwright Ahead of Her Time

Early March invites a false spring
of blossoming and blooming, the grooming
of pink peonies into flaunting their frothy
frou-frou

until one night the frost comes,
penning its coldness on the petals
like a cruel critic, parsing
each peony from its stalk.

I see the flowerheads in the morning lying, dying
on the greenish pavement, but later
it seems that someone has rescued them
from being trampled underfoot.

The inflorescences are sitting on a wall,
blazing their final defiant pinkness,
taking their last frivolous bow
in the rapturous applause of the sun.

Like I Was Never There

As the first swirling spits of sleet descend
we arrive at the Limelight and order pints of Snow Beer,
its froth like a dimpled layer of snow on top.

The lights are blizzarding on the dance floor
and you ask if you can take me home,
looking at me with longing eyes
but when we go outside it's snowing,
taking the heat out of our thoughts,
snowing hard in diagonals, wind scything
through the city streets and I score a lift with a small-time
DJ instead who drops me at the corner of my road.

The snow is blowing up the walls,
pebble-dashing them white.
I can hear the soft swish of slush from cars
and in the distance, the tinny flap of a letterbox.
The snow is layering the leaves of a holly bush
like ascending vertebrae, jagged ice sculptures
forming on the kerb weeds.

At one point I stop and look back,
the compressed black treadmark of my shoe
greying, filling in, whitening, like I was
never there. And then, I see a heart shape
made from tiny footprints
and I think of you as every second
blurs the white edges of the black night.

The next morning the world is full of the
crunch of swiftly moving boots chanting,
I should have stayed with you,
I should have gone with you,
I should have been with you.

Tufts of green shimmy through the icefields
of Ormeau Park, a waterfall from a melting
chimney pot weed running down the side of a house;
the world is amelt, svelte with flow,
snow avalanching down the windscreens.

A faint glimmer of sunlight plays cruelly with me
lighting up the lines on my face, making me look
older, while everything around me is beautiful,
though you are not here to see it.

The snow is humped on low bushes like the duveted
bodies of rough sleepers. The brown ferns begin to
show through the snow on the hills,
aping the tones of Presbyterian sandstone.

The crystalline snow turns opaque, ice-cubed at its
margins, dissolving, neither snow nor water.
The thought of you embodies me just for one second
and then I fracture along my icy edges,
detaching, retreating, sliding in a subglacial dream –
clouds fuming through the Cave Hill cliffs,
white Lagan, white sky, white snow
like I was never there.

BREXIT

That spring was the bitterest seen in an age.
The daffodils were bombarded,
torn, blasted by the winds,
weighed down, crushed by snow.
They were prostrate, kissing the ground
with a corona of puckered lips,
whispering to the earth to let them back in.

The Gun that Shot John Caldwell

He unearthed the gun on a path near Bloody Bridge,
marked by a pine roped with vines,
brightened with lichen, on an incline lined
with a staircase of roots. The fallen needles
were a bloody rust, meshed like flesh,
as he sliced through the mud with a spade.
Walking back to the car
the coloured hats lost by lone hikers
were hanging from the branches, reminding him
of pagan tributes to the sylvan gods,
a wishing tree of Eó Mughna.

The day after he shot John Caldwell
but failed to kill him
he couldn't free his mind of the bondaged pine
or those woven fruits strung along the trees.
He went back to the bridge to hide his gun
and looked out to the sea,
a silvery strip of sun on the horizon
and the iron ore river, in awe of the force of it,
of how it was so strong, it would cut through granite,
so strong, it would cut through history.

The 6a to the River of Lethe

The skinny teen is sitting hooded under the brow
of the 6a bus stop and a grey hypnotised sky,
wasted as the waste ground that lies behind him,
sucking weed smoke through a breath-shivered bag.

The rest of us are awaiting the next bus
while he waits for his next buzz and, after a time,
he rises and wanders in a daze onto the tattered land
through ankle-turning rocks and meadowsweet.

An indigent in a tracksuit two sizes too big for him,
he throws away his plastic bag, searching for new ones
suspended in the flowers of the buddleia bush
like fruit ripened by the wind, and strangely

when we look up at the electric sign, it says,
'Diversion due to roadworks. The 6a will now be going
to Lemosyne. We apologise for any inconvenience.'
The boy's aromatic smoke still lingers, fingers the air,
sending up clouds to the amethyst ether.

Summer Salt

One last hump of the sleepered path
and there it is, Murlough, the sea in full flood,
in full-throated swell under the cloudy blue sky,
the sun reflecting a big pool of light
like a flattened circle out at sea, while tipping
the crests of incoming waves,
gleaming off the wet stone at the shore's edge.

The bulbous sclerous eyes stare at us
from the foam as pebbles are dragged back
into the surf with a hard basalt rumble.
I pick up the white test of a heart urchin
and it's a miracle it's untouched amidst the clattering
boulders – like a heart that can survive anything.

The tide keeps trying to tag our feet,
mischievously keeping us on our toes, so we
sit on the sunlit sand on the lip of the dunes
and look out to the white marbling on the waves,
hearing the whisper of the thatched marram
while the gorse flutes a Percy French air
at our backs, vying with the thunderous ocean.

Beside us, the sandhoppers flip their amber bodies
and perform wild feats of seaside gymnastics
and, just then, something in my chest skips,
flips over for ever, somersaults.
Ah yes, summer salts
onto my tongue.

Pommel Horse
for Rhys McClenaghan

He slaps the horse's hide
into plumes of white floury chalk
as his hands pirouette on the smallest stage,
his skin patting the leather
until he grips the pommels, and feet
pointed like a ballerina in the air,
he spins, scissors, spindles and flares.
The suspense is in the fractions
between victory and defeat – one slip
of the hand and it's almost out of his grasp;
a gasp, but he arcs and arrows,
circling five times like five Olympic rings,
and with one last swing of the hips
traces the shape of a golden medal
and handstands into a land of blind belief.

Acknowledgements

Thanks to Alan Hayes who published me in 3 volumes of *Washing Windows* and was instrumental in the forging of these poems. Thanks also to Damian Smyth and the Arts Council of Northern Ireland for their ongoing support which is truly appreciated. Thanks to the Arts Council of Ireland who granted me an Agility Award. I'd like to thank Barry Kerr and all those who inspired me to write the poems: the blessed and the damned, the indigent and the grand and the craziest pack of bastards in the land.

Various iterations of these poems have appeared in the following publications:
'Madden's Bar, Castle Court' in *The Lonely Poets' Guide to Belfast*.
'Sandy Row Riots' in *Washing Windows Too* (Arlen House).
'Orchardlands' in *Poetry Ireland Review*.
'Oceanus' in *Romance Options* (Dedalus Press).
'After Daniel McColgan's Murder' in *Acumen*.
'Noah Donohoe' in *Journey Turas Raik* (New Isles Press).
'Axis Mundi' in *Washing Windows III* (Arlen House).
'A Belfast Summer' in *Poetry Ireland Review*.
'Heliophile' in *Washing Windows IV* (Arlen House).

'Pommel Horse' was published for Poetry Day 2024 by Poetry Ireland.

About the Author

Rosemary Jenkinson is a playwright, poet and fiction writer from Belfast. She taught English in Greece, France, the Czech Republic and Poland before returning to Belfast in 2002. Her plays include *The Bonefire* (Stewart Parker BBC Radio Award), *Planet Belfast, Here Comes the Night, Michelle and Arlene, May the Road Rise Up* and *Lives in Translation*. Her plays have been performed in Dublin, London, Edinburgh, Brussels, New York, Washington DC and Belfast. Arlen House publish her latest plays *Billy Boy* (2022) and *Silent Trade* (2023). *Manichea*, her play about censorship in publishing, is forthcoming in 2025.

In 2018 she received a Major Artist Award from the Arts Council of Northern Ireland. She has been writer-in-residence at the Lyric Theatre Belfast, the Leuven Centre for Irish Studies and the Irish Cultural Centre in Paris. Her short story collections include *Contemporary Problems Nos. 53 & 54, Aphrodite's Kiss, Catholic Boy* (shortlisted for the EU Prize for Literature), *Lifestyle Choice 10mgs* (shortlisted for the Edge Hill Short Story Prize), *Marching Season* and *Love in the Time of Chaos* (shortlisted for the Edge Hill Short Story Prize). She is currently Royal Literary Fund Fellow at Queen's University.

The Irish Times has praised her for 'an elegant wit, terrific characterisation and an absolute sense of her own particular Belfast'.